World of Faiths

Hinduism

Anita Ganeri

QED Publishing

Copyright © QED Publishing 2006

First published in the UK in 2006 by
QED Publishing
A Quarto Group company
226 City Road
London EC1V 2TT
www.qed-publishing.co.uk

Reprinted in 2007

A catalogue record for this book is available from the British Library.

ISBN 978 1 84538 709 9

Written by Anita Ganeri
Designed by Tall Tree Books
Editor Louisa Somerville
Consultant John Keast

Publisher Steve Evans
Creative Director Zeta Davies
Editorial Director Jean Coppendale

Printed and bound in China

Picture credits To follow
Key: t = top, b = bottom, c = centre, l = left, r = right, FC = front cover

Ark Religion /Helene Rogers 5t 5b, 7t, 8t 8b, 9t, 11t 11b, 12, 13t 13b, 14, 16, 21b, 25b, 27b /Peter Rauter title
page, 24 /Robin Graham 4; **Dinodia Photo Library** 6, 10, 21t, 25t /Fiona Good 7b, 15b, 17t, 20, 23t /Andrea
Alborno 15t; **Trip** 22 /Adina Tovey 26 /Robin Smith 27t.

Website information is correct at the time of going to press.
However, the publishers cannot accept liability for any
information or links found on third-party websites.

Words in **bold** are explained
in the glossary on page 30.

Contents

What is Hinduism?

Hinduism is the religion that is followed by people called Hindus. Most Hindus do not use the name 'Hinduism'. They call their religion **sanatana dharma**, or 'eternal teaching'. Eternal means something that lasts forever. Hindus believe that this teaching has always been true and will be true forever. Hindus believe that this teaching applies to everyone, in all places and at all times. You can find out more about Hindu beliefs throughout this book.

The start of Hinduism

Hinduism began in India and is one of the oldest religions in the world. It goes back at least 5,000 years to the time of the great Indus Valley Civilization in northern India. Its people worshipped many gods and goddesses similar to those that Hindus worship today. Many stone seals (used for stamping a mark or symbol) have been found at the site, showing **sacred** animals such as elephants.

▼ The ancient ruins of Mohenjo Daro, one of the greatest of the Indus Valley cities.

Hinduism expands

About 3,500 years ago, the Aryan people from central Asia moved into northern India and spread out through the country. They brought their own religious ideas and their beliefs became mixed with those of the Indus people. Hindus still worship some of the Aryan gods, such as Agni, the god of fire, and read the Aryan sacred texts, including the Vedas (see page 16).

▲ The god Agni has been important in the Hindu religion since ancient times.

Sacred ceremonies

The Aryans performed many complicated **rituals** to keep the gods happy. By doing this, they hoped that the gods would grant them favours such as good health or a large harvest. During the rituals, the priest threw offerings of grains, spices and butter into a sacred fire. It was believed that the flames would carry the offerings up to the gods.

▲ This is the Om symbol. Om is a sacred sound, which is pronounced 'aum'.

Sacred symbol

The Om symbol represents a sacred sound. Hindus believe that it is the sound by which the whole universe was created. All other sounds, including speech, came from it. The sound 'Om' is chanted at the start and end of Hindu prayers, and during meditation (see page 15). The symbol is also used to decorate **mandirs** (Hindu temples).

Hindu beliefs

Hindus can follow their religion in many different ways, but most Hindus share the same beliefs. Many Hindus believe in a great spirit beyond the world we can see around us. They call this spirit 'Brahman'. **Brahman** cannot be seen but is everywhere. Everything is what it is because Brahman is in it. Some Hindus call Brahman 'God'.

Rebirth

Hindus believe that every living thing has a **soul**. When you die, your soul is reborn in another body and so you live on after death. This new body may be an animal, a plant or a human being. You can be reborn again and again in a continuous cycle of suffering and misery. Hindus hope to stop this happening by leading good lives. Then they can break free and become one with Brahman. Breaking free is called moksha.

◀ A Hindu boys reads the sacred texts to learn more about his religion.

Karma

The way you live this life causes your next life to be better, worse or the same. If you lead a good life, you will have a good life next time. If you lead a bad life, your next life will be hard. This is called **karma**, an Indian word for action. Karma means your actions (good or bad) and the consequences, or results, of those actions (good or bad).

▲ For Hindus, cows are sacred animals. This one has been dressed up for a festival.

"My religion is very important to me. It's part of my everyday life. It means loving God, not hurting any living things, being honest and working as hard as I can."

◀ Children on their way to school. Working hard is an important part of the Hindu religion.

7

Gods and goddesses

Hindus believe in one God, but they also **worship** many other gods and goddesses who show Brahman's different forms and qualities. There are hundreds of gods and goddesses in Hinduism. Some are more popular than others or are thought to be more important. Hindus usually choose a god to worship that their family worships or who they feel has helped them in some way.

► The goddess Parvati. She is Shiva's wife and mother of Ganesha, the elephant-headed god.

Principal gods

The three main gods are Brahma who created the world, Vishnu who protects the world and Shiva who destroys the world. Hindus do not often worship Brahma today, but Vishnu and Shiva have many followers. The most important goddess is called Shakti, Shiva's wife. She can be fierce and frightening, or gentle and kind. In her fierce form, she is called Kali. In her gentle form, she is called Parvati.

► Hindus offer garlands to God – and to guests – as a sign of welcome.

Krishna and Rama

Two of the best-loved Hindu gods are Krishna and Rama. They are both forms of Lord Vishnu, and are worshipped all over India. Krishna is more mischievous and likes to play tricks. His story is part of a poem called the Mahabharata (see page 17). The god Rama is worshipped as a hero and king. His story is told in another poem, called the Ramayana (see pages 17 and 18–19).

▲ Krishna is often worshipped with his wife Radha. He is often shown with *blue* skin to show that he is holy and playing a flute.

Hanuman

Another popular god is Hanuman, the monkey warrior and servant of Lord Rama. He is worshipped alongside Rama but he is also worshipped on his own as God's servant. He is famous for his courage and strength. Soldiers and sportspeople pray to him to help them find the same qualities.

Make a garland of welcome

You will need: different-coloured tissue paper • pencil • ruler • scissors • sticky tape • needle and thread

1 Cut out 15 20 x 20cm squares from different-coloured tissue paper. With your finger, gently push down the middle of one square and make a flower shape.

2 Pinch the tissue paper under the petals and then twist the rest into a stem. Wrap sticky tape around the stem to hold it together.

3 Cut a straight line across the petals. Make 14 more flowers, then ask an adult to push a needle and thread through all of the stems to finish the garland.

Hindu worship

any Hindus go to worship in a place called a mandir. It is sometimes called a temple. There are no fixed rules for when Hindus should go. Some Hindus try to visit the mandir every day on their way to work or school. Others only go at special times, such as festivals and family celebrations. Hindus can visit the mandir on their own or with other people. Sometimes a whole family will arrange an outing to a particularly important mandir. A mandir may be a small shrine on a street corner, or a large, grandly decorated building.

Sacred images

For Hindus, the mandir is God's home on earth. Each mandir is dedicated to a god or goddess, or another holy person. A **murti** (sacred image) of the god stands in the main **shrine**, often with other murtis beside it. This is the holiest part of the mandir. Hindus believe that murtis show God's presence on earth.

◀ Sacred images of Rama, his wife Sita and his brother Lakshman. The monkey god, Hanuman, is kneeling at Rama's feet.

In the home

Most Hindus also worship at home. They set aside a room, or part of a room, as a shrine. Here they put an image of their favourite god or goddess. Many Hindus worship in the morning, when the house is quiet and before the hustle and bustle of the day begins.

▲ A small shrine in a Hindu's home. The family say their prayers here every day.

▲ These worshippers in Singapore are barefoot, ready to go inside the mandir.

"When I visit the mandir, I take off my shoes to show respect to God. It also helps keep the mandir pure and clean. I also put my hands together as a way of greeting God. Then I ring the mandir bell to show that I have arrived!"

Brahma mandir

There are many mandirs dedicated to the gods Shiva and Vishnu. But the only mandir dedicated to Brahma is in the town of Pushkar in western India. An image of a goose stands at its entrance. The goose is Brahma's special animal and it is said that it chose the site on which the mandir was built.

11

Visiting a mandir

Hindu worship is called **puja**. This means 'giving respect'. When Hindus worship, they go to see the murtis (see page 10) in the shrine to receive their blessing. They say prayers and make offerings of flowers, fruit, rice and money. The flowers and money are used in worship. The food is offered to the murtis to be **blessed** by God. Then it becomes **prasad** (sacred food). Some of it is handed back to the worshippers in order to give them God's blessing.

Welcoming God

The main ceremony of worship in a mandir is called **arti**. It is used to welcome the murtis. The priest takes a tray of lamps and waves it in a circle in front of the images for God's blessing. As he does so, the worshippers sing a song of praise to show their love for God. Then they pass their hands over the flames and touch their foreheads.

▼ Puja taking place in a Hindu temple around a sacred fire.

The elephant god

Ganesha is the god with an elephant's head. He is the god of new beginnings and is believed to take away difficulties. Hindus pray to Ganesha before they begin worship or any new task. Ganesha is the son of the god Shiva and the goddess Parvati. Legend says that Parvati made him out of clay. Images of Ganesha are often painted over doorways so that he will bless the household.

▲ Children in a mandir in Britain holding offerings of fruit.

▶ Ganesha holds a broken pen in one of his right hands. It is said he broke it while writing a very long poem called the Mahabarata (*see page 17*).

Hindu prayer

This is a prayer that Hindus say to Ganesha:
'O Lord Ganesha, With a curved trunk And large body, Shining with the brilliance Of a million suns. Please take away all obstacles From my good actions.'

Priests and holy people

Every Hindu mandir has at least one priest. Some large mandirs have many priests. The priest performs puja (see page 12) and other ceremonies, such as weddings and funerals. He helps people to read and understand the sacred texts. But the priest's main job is to look after the murtis (see page 10). They are treated as if they are honoured guests. The priest wakes them up in the morning, washes and dresses them, and gives them breakfast. The murtis rest in the afternoon. In the evening, the priest dresses them in their nightclothes, ready to go to bed.

Home visits

On special occasions, priests also visit people at home. This may happen after a baby is born. The priest uses the time and place of the baby's birth to write a chart called a **horoscope**. The horoscope is used later to work out the best dates for events in the person's life, such as their wedding day.

◀ A Hindu priest in Mauritius with his hands together in greeting.

Holy men

Some priests lead very strict lives. They are called **sadhus** (holy men). They take vows not to get married, or to have any money or belongings of their own. They give up their homes and families, and try to stay free from selfish feelings, such as anger and pride.

▲ A Hindu holy man meditating.

▲ A priest performing puja in a mandir.

'In life and in death, in happiness and in misery, God is equally present. The whole world is full of God. Open your eyes and see God.'
Swami Vivekananda (1863-1902)

Meditation

Meditation is an important part of Hindu worship. It helps Hindus to make their minds calm and to see God living in their hearts. Many Hindus chant a short prayer, called a **mantra**, over and over again to help them to focus their minds.

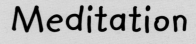

15

Sacred texts

Hindus have many different sacred texts. The oldest are called the Vedas. They include prayers, hymns and instructions for how to worship. The first Veda is called the Rig Veda (Song of Knowledge). It was probably composed over 3,000 years ago. Priests recite verses from the Vedas at many Hindu ceremonies, including weddings. The Vedas and Upanishads (see below) are called shruti or 'heard' texts. It is believed that a group of wise men heard these texts directly from God. The Mahabharata and the Ramayana (see opposite) are called shrmriti or 'remembered' texts. These were composed by people, learned by heart and passed on.

Ancient texts

Another set of texts is called the Upanishads. They may be over 2,500 years old. They talk about the relationship between people and God. The name Upanishad means 'sit down near'. Long ago, pupils used to sit down on the ground near their **gurus** (religious teachers) to listen to them speak.

◄ A priest reading from the sacred texts in a mandir. Priests help worshippers to understand the meaning of the texts.

Popular poems

Two very long poems are also part of the Hindu sacred texts. They are called the Mahabharata and the Ramayana. The Mahabarata tells the story of a quarrel between two royal families. The most important part of the poem is called the Bhagavad Gita (Song of the Lord). It tells how the god Krishna teaches a prince from one of the royal families about the right way to live and worship. The Ramayana tells the story of how Prince Rama rescues his wife, Sita, from an evil demon king. You can read this story on pages 18–19.

▲ The story of the Ramayana shown in pictures on a temple wall in South India.

Hindu storybook

Read the story of Rama and Sita on the next two pages. Then make a storybook and write your own version of the story in it. Think about the story and the message it contains. What special qualities do the main characters show? For example, Hanuman is brave and a loyal friend. Can you think of any times in your own life when you have helped out a friend, just as Hanuman came to Rama's rescue?

The story of Rama and Sita

Long ago, Prince Rama was born in Ayodhya, in India, where his father was the king. Rama was the king's favourite son and his father wanted Rama to be king after him. But Rama's stepmother wanted her own son to be king instead. So she sent Rama to live in a distant forest with his wife, Sita, and his brother, Lakshman.

Many years passed. One day, Rama and Lakshman went out hunting for a golden deer. While they were gone, a terrible thing happened. Sita was kidnapped by Ravana, the wicked, ten-headed demon king of the island of Lanka. Laughing from each of his ten terrible mouths, he carried her off to his palace, far, far away.

For days, Rama and Lakshman searched the forest but they could not find Sita anywhere. Then Rama had an idea. He called on his friend, the monkey general, Hanuman, for help. With a huge army of monkeys and bears, they set off for Lanka to rescue Sita. Ravana was ready for them, with his own gruesome army of giants and demons. The two armies fought fiercely, and finally, Rama and Ravana came face to face. Quick as a flash, Rama killed Ravana with a golden arrow, given to him by the gods.

Rama and Sita were reunited and went back home to Ayodhya to be crowned king and queen.

Holy places

ach year, millions of Hindus make special journeys, called **pilgrimages**, to holy places. They believe that visiting a holy place will help them to break free from being reborn. Some people also go to pray for something special, such as good health. Many of these places are linked to events in the lives of the gods and goddesses, or are famous for their beauty or healing qualities. Pilgrims travel by plane, train, boat or cart. Some even go on foot, though the journey may take several days to complete.

Shiva's home

The holiest place for Hindus is the city of Varanasi in northern India. A legend says that the god, Shiva, chose Varanasi to be his home on Earth. Millions of **pilgrims** flock to the city to visit the hundreds of mandirs and to bathe in the River Ganges. The river is sacred to Hindus. They believe that bathing in the river's water will wash away their sins.

◄ Gangotri, high up in the Himalayan mountains, is the source of the sacred River Ganges.

Holy waters

Every 12 years, millions of pilgrims visit the city of Allahabad. This is the place where the holy River Ganges, the River Yamuna and the mythical River Saraswati all flow together. The pilgrims come to bathe in the water. A huge, temporary camp is set up to house everyone.

◀ The Golden Temple in Varanasi is dedicated to Lord Shiva. It is the holiest mandir in the city.

▲ Pilgrims bathing in the river at Allahabad. This gathering is called the Kumbh Mela fair.

"For Hindus like me, Varanasi is a holy city. We call it a **tirtha** (crossing place). We believe that it's a place where you can cross over from this world to freedom from being reborn. It's a very special place for me and I try to make a pilgrimage there every year."

21

Family celebrations

Family life is very important for Hindus. There are many special times in a Hindu's life when the whole family gets together to celebrate. Sometimes, celebrations take place in the mandir. Sometimes, the priest visits the family at home.

Birth

The birth of a baby is a happy time. When the baby is about 12 days old, a ceremony is held at which it is given its name. The baby's father or the priest recites a prayer for the baby's health and happiness. The priest also draws the baby's horoscope (see page 14).

Weddings

At a Hindu wedding ceremony, a priest guides the couple through the prayers and rituals. The ceremony takes place around a sacred fire. The bride and groom take seven steps together. With each step, they promise each other good health, wealth, friendship and so on.

► At their wedding, the bride and groom throw offerings into the sacred fire.

Thread ceremony

When a Hindu boy is about ten years old, a special ceremony marks the end of his childhood and the start of his adult life. He is given a sacred thread which he wears looped over his left shoulder. He must wear the thread all the time, for the rest of his life.

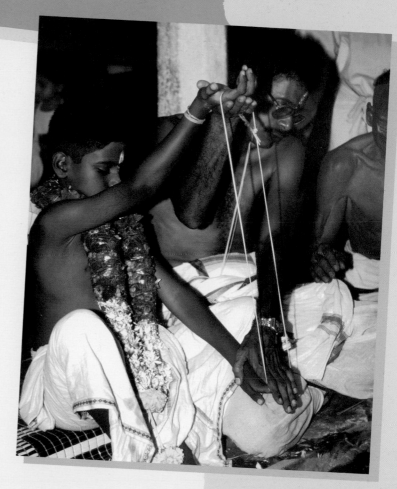

▶ A Hindu boy is given his sacred thread by his father.

Make a bookmark

You will need: card • pencil • scissors • red felt tip pen

A Hindu bride has her hands decorated with a red dye called mehndi.

1 Draw around each of your hands onto card and then carefully cut out both of the hand shapes.

2 Draw three lines on each hand shape for fingers. Use a red felt-tip pen to decorate the hands. You can design your own patterns or use the ones shown here.

3 Use your decorated card hands as bookmarks. Or you could stick them on the wall or give them to friends as special cards.

23

Festival time

There are hundreds of Hindu festivals throughout the year. Celebrations include a special puja, music and dancing, and giving cards and gifts. The two most important festivals are Divali and Holi. They are celebrated by Hindus all over the world. These are lively, happy times when whole communities join in the celebrations. Many festivals remember important events in the lives of the gods.

Festival of lights

Divali falls in October or November. In India, it lasts for five days. In Britain and other countries, Hindus often celebrate on the nearest weekend. Divali is the festival of lights. Hindus remember the story of Rama and Sita (see pages 18–19), and light divas (lamps) to welcome them home. Some Hindus hold a puja in honour of Lakshmi, the goddess of wealth and good luck.

▼ Women float oil lamps on a lake to celebrate Divali.

24

Spring festival

Holi is the festival which marks the end of winter and the beginning of spring. It is the time when farmers traditionally celebrated the first harvest of spring. Holi gets its name from a witch called Holika. A story tells how Holika tried to kill her nephew because he worshipped Vishnu, but was killed instead. On the night before Holi, people light bonfires and burn models of Holika.

▲ A blazing bonfire lit for Holi.

▲ Children getting drenched in coloured water is part of the Holi fun.

Raksha bandhan

Raksha bandhan is a festival that takes place in August. Sisters tie brightly coloured bracelets, called rakhis, around their brothers' wrists. They ask their brothers to look after them in the coming year. In return, the brothers must give their sisters a gift.

25

Around the world

Today, there are about 1,000 million Hindus in the world. Most Hindus live in India, where Hinduism began. In fact, eight out of ten people in India are Hindus. Hindus also live in other Asian countries, such as Nepal, Sri Lanka and Malaysia, and in Africa and the Caribbean. More recently, Hindus have gone to live in Europe and North America.

Hindus in Britain

About 400,000 Hindus live in Britain. They mostly come from the Punjab in north-west India and Gujarat in west India. Many of them came to live in Britain between the 1950s and 1970s. Today, there are some 150 Hindu mandirs in Britain. They are important places for Hindus to meet as well as to worship. Some mandirs have been newly built. Others have been set up in other buildings, such as churches and school halls.

▼ The beautiful Swaminarayan Mandir in Neasden, London, was built in 1995. Its design is in a traditional style and it is covered in beautiful carvings.

"I live in Singapore. We have our own temple in the city. It's very beautiful. Nearby, there are lots of shops and stalls selling silk for making saris, and all sorts of spices. It's almost like being in India!"

▶ Dancers in Bali acting out the story of the Ramayana (*see pages 18–19*).

Balinese Hindus

On the island of Bali in Indonesia, most of the people (about three million) are Hindus. Hinduism was first brought to Bali about 1,800 years ago by traders from India. Later, a Hindu king from nearby Java conquered the island. There are many ancient mandirs on the island, and colourful dances and puppet shows are used to tell stories from the sacred texts.

▼ Hindu children in Britain studying Indian languages at a class held at their mandir.

Learning about Hinduism

Wherever they live, it is important for Hindu children to learn about their religion. Some mandirs run classes where children can learn to read and study the Hindu sacred texts. Many of these texts are written in **Sanskrit**, an ancient Indian language that is extremely difficult to learn.

Activity

Make a finger-puppet Divali theatre

You will need: tracing paper • pencil • thin white card • ruler • black ball-point pen • coloured pencils • scissors • sticky tape • cardboard box • craft knife • different-coloured tissue paper • glue • thin coloured card • sequins

Turn back to pages 18-19 and read the story of Rama and Sita. In India, it is often acted out by travelling actors and with puppets, especially during the festival of Divali (see page 24). Find out here how to put on a finger-puppet show. You could write a play based on the story. Then use a computer to print out copies of the script for your friends.

1 In pencil, trace or copy each of the five characters below onto thin white card. Leave 2cm spaces between them.

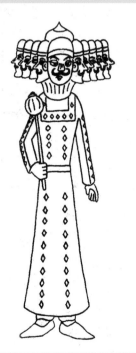

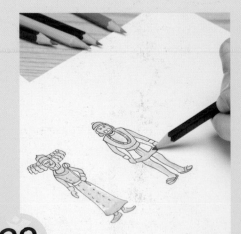

2 Go over your drawings with a black ball-point pen. Use coloured pencils to colour in each character.

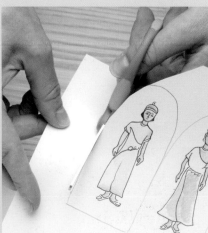

3 In pencil, draw an arched-topped rectangle around each character and then cut each rectangle out.

4 Draw round one of the cut-out characters onto thin white card five times. Cut them all out. Use sticky tape to attach one to the *back* of each of the five characters. Don't tape along the bottom – that's where your finger will go!

5 Ask an adult to cut away the top flaps and bottom of a cardboard box. Glue different-coloured tissue paper all over the outside and inside of the box.

6 Cut out a rectangle from coloured card that's bigger than your box. Copy the shape of the stage front below onto the card and then cut it out.

7 Glue sequins all over your stage front for decoration. Stand the cardboard box on its side and attach the stage front using sticky tape.

8 Place the box on the edge of a table. Kneel behind it and put your puppets on your fingers. It's showtime!

Glossary

arti A ceremony of worship. Objects, such as lamps and incense, are offered to the sacred images of the gods and goddesses.

blessed When an object or person is made holy and will then be looked after by God.

Brahman The great spirit that is beyond the everyday world. Some Hindus call Brahman 'God'.

gurus Holy teachers.

horoscope A chart drawn up for a Hindu baby. It shows the position of the moon, stars and planets at the time of the baby's birth.

karma An Indian word meaning 'action'. It means people's good and bad actions and the good and bad results of these actions.

mandir A building where Hindus worship. Mandirs are sometimes called temples.

mantra A short prayer that is recited over and over again by Hindus when they are meditating.

meditation A type of worship in which a person clears and calms their mind in order that they can concentrate better on God.

murti A sacred image of a god or goddess that is the main focus of Hindu worship. Hindus believe that God is present in the murti.

pilgrimages Journeys to sacred places, such as mountains and rivers.

pilgrim A person who goes on a pilgrimage.

prasad Sacred food. This is food that has been offered to the gods and goddesses for their blessing, then is shared out among the worshippers.

puja The main Hindu form of worship in which people make offerings to the gods and goddesses. Puja means 'giving respect'.

rituals Religious ceremonies.

sacred Another word for holy.

sadhus Hindu holy men who give up their homes and possessions to dedicate themselves to God.

sanatana dharma 'Eternal teaching'. This is the name that Hindus give to their beliefs, rather than Hinduism.

Sanskrit An ancient Indian language that is the sacred language of Hinduism.

shrine Part of a mandir or a place at home where the murtis stand and puja is performed.

soul A word used for the thinking, feeling part of a person, rather than the person's physical body.

tirtha A crossing place. A place, such as a sacred river, where Hindus believe that you can cross from this world into freedom from being born again.

worship A way of praising God.

Index

Notes for parents and teachers

Religions guidelines

This book is an accessible introduction to the beliefs and practices of the Hindu faith. It does not aim to be a comprehensive guide but gives plenty of opportunity for further activities and study. The content is closely linked to the non-statutory framework for Religious Education, particularly the QCA schemes of work listed below. The topics selected also overlap with locally agreed RE syllabuses.

Unit 1A: What does it mean to belong?

Unit 1D: Beliefs and practice

Unit 2C: Celebrations

Unit 2D: Visiting a place of worship

Unit 3A: What do signs and symbols mean in religion?

Unit 3B: How and why do Hindus celebrate Divali?

Unit 4A: How and why do Hindus worship at home and in the mandir?

Unit 4D: What religions are represented in our neighbourhood?

Unit 6A: Worship and community

Unit 6C: Why are sacred texts important?

Visiting a mandir

A good way to gain an insight into what being a Hindu means is to visit a mandir. Many mandirs welcome visitors, as long as you follow certain rules of behaviour. Find out where your local mandir is and phone in advance to arrange a time to visit.

Visitors should dress sensibly and observe all the customs and traditions. For example, you must take off your shoes before you enter the mandir (there is usually a shoe store where you can leave them). Women and girls may be expected to cover their heads. Ask permission if you want to take photographs - these will probably not be allowed inside the mandir.

At the end of the visit, a good way of saying thank you is to make a small donation to the mandir funds.

To make the most of your visit, write down a checklist of things to look out for in the mandir and questions to ask beforehand.

More books to read

Keystones: Hindu Mandir
Anita Ganeri, A & C Black 2000

Sacred texts: the Ramayana
Anita Ganeri, Evans Brothers 2003

Religions of the World: Hinduism
Sue Penney, Heinemann Library 2002

Celebrations: Divali
Anita Ganeri, Heinemann Library 2001

Useful websites

www.hindunet.org
A useful site for general information about Hinduism.

www.indiancultureonline.com
Another general site.

www.hindukids.org
A site written for young readers with lots of information about Hinduism, including fun animations.

www.swaminarayan.org
The website of the beautiful Swaminarayan Mandir in London, Britain.